Chapter 1
The Restaurant Business

Whether you are a server, a cook, a host, a manager, or a bartender, the restaurant business is very stressful. You have to constantly deal with the needs and wants of internal and external guests. You have your dining customer, your boss, your co-workers, your delivery people, your repair people, and so on. You could find yourself dealing with an unhappy customer, an angry boss, a bitchy co-worker, a late delivery, and broken equipment all on one shift. So why does one work in the restaurant business?

It is very easy to get a job in the restaurant industry. Turnover at restaurants is usually high, leading to jobs always being available. Anyone with a good smile and attitude can get a server job. Looking a little rough around the edges? You can be a cook. Are you a gorgeous female? How does hosting sound? Most people get a job in the restaurant business to fill the void in your wallet. Sadly, most get stuck in a job they considered temporary.

My first job was at a restaurant in 1993 at a place called Tom Wahl's in Avon, NY. I worked there from age fourteen until I turned sixteen. I had no clue about the industry, or what I was even doing. Luckily, this place had managers that cared and helped young kids. I didn't know how to deal with an angry customer. There were probably times I didn't even know that one was upset. This job introduced me to serving food and that was about it. I was too immature to understand. I had to fill the void in my wallet to buy Sega Genesis games. The food, by the way, is phenomenal. If you ever find yourself in upstate NY, stop at Tom Wahl's.

I left the food service industry until 2004 when once again I found myself trying to fill a void in my wallet. This time it was to pay rent and bills (and buy PlayStation 2 games.) This temporary job led me to nine more years in restaurants, climbing the ladder from server to General Manager. So why is it so hard to get out of this business?

Familiarity at a job keeps you stable. You do what you know how to do. Serving people comes naturally. When one restaurant doesn't work out, the easiest thing to do is go to the one next door. It's called following the path of least resistance. All you have to do is learn a new menu because the basics are the same. You may also have former coworkers who took this path and string you along. Besides, it is hard to switch industries when all your resume has on it is restaurants.

If you have never worked a day in a restaurant in your entire life, then I hope this book is very educational for you. If you are a rude customer, then I hope this book changes your outlook. If you currently work in a restaurant and despise your job, I hope this book motivates you to follow whatever dream you had in the first place when you took your "temporary job."

"Working in restaurants sucks because of poor wages, moody customers, and over demanding superiors. If the C.E.O. was more concerned with customer service than the bottom line, maybe the business would be able to show that they are actually more concerned with the customer than the bottom line."

- Robert Evans, former sub maker

Chapter 2
The Customer

The customer is always right. We've all heard it, and we all know it's bullshit. The restaurant industry follows this motto tighter than any other business in America. If a customer is upset about something, you better fix it, and fast.

People act differently when they are at a restaurant than they would if they were out shopping at a place like Wal-Mart. (I use Wal-Mart as an example a lot in the book because I worked there for seven years and had a good time.) When you are greeted at Wal-Mart, you aren't taken to a particular aisle. You just go on your merry way and do your shopping. Imagine hearing "Hello, welcome to Wal-Mart. Follow me to automotive." Silly, right? Not in sit-down restaurants. The host takes you to your destination. They take you where they are supposed to by rotating sections for servers. When done properly, this helps servers make equal money and not get "double or triple sat." That means they get two or three tables in quick succession, which for the most part raises their stress level and lowers their service ability. This will happen when a customer says "I don't want to sit here. I want to sit in a booth by a window." The host usually smiles, and then brings them to their desired table and gets a nasty look from the server. What is wrong with just taking the table you are given? Why do customers have to be so picky? Next time you get a tire rotation, tell the mechanics exactly the order you want your tires removed in. Tell your dentist which teeth to clean first. "I don't want you to start with my front teeth. I want you to start with my molars." I could go on with examples, but you get the point.

Ever go to Wal-Mart and see that your favorite cereal has gone up in price? Do you hunt down an associate and bitch about it? God forbid coffee goes up ten cents in a restaurant. It's like the end of the world. Society understands that insurance prices go up each year. They understand that cigarette prices are always increasing. Society expects restaurants to never raise their prices. Customers get very evil about this. I've heard customers tell their server that the difference is coming out of their tip. Yes, Mr. Evil Customer, this particular server made the decision to raise the menu prices company wide. Wake up.

There are several reasons why restaurants, along with every other business in America, raise their prices. One of the main reasons is the customer. Restaurants give so many discounts or free food to unhappy guests. The math isn't hard. The money has to be recuperated somehow. Why do so many customers complain? Because they know they will get free food. Next time you see a bad movie, ask for a refund when you leave. You'll be laughed out of the building. Restaurants have collectively entered this trend of doing anything and everything to satisfy an angry customer. I wish I knew who started this trend so I could slap them in the face. It's a trend you can't get out of. I've tried it. I had a customer that I knew was lying. He ate his entire meal, and said it was cold and disgusting. I apologized and told him if he had said something to his server earlier in the meal, we could have fixed it. He wanted me to take the entire meal off the check. I wouldn't do it. The man went home and called the corporate office. They sent him $25.

Restaurants will give discounts or free food for just about any complaint. I was told at one of my jobs that if the food takes longer than twenty-five minutes I should just buy the whole check. Say what? Waiting twenty-five minutes at a sit-down restaurant during a busy time is not a long wait. Go wait in line at Wal-Mart for twenty-five minutes and ask for a discount because you waited so long. They would think you are the local comedian. Not at a restaurant. You probably just earned a free meal.

Would you have preferred to get your food faster and not have it cooked all the way? Would you like me to ask the other fifteen tables ahead of you if they would let us cook your food first? Many times on the job I would have loved to ask those questions. It doesn't matter what is going on around them, most customers just want their food as fast as possible. No wonder we have a weight epidemic in America. We're a nation full of hungry, hungry hippos.

People on lunch break are the worst when it comes to complaining about waiting for their food. "I only have a thirty minute lunch break. I need my food fast." Why, if you only have thirty minutes, would you go to a sit down restaurant? These assholes need to pack their lunch or go get fast food. I had a group of four women who would come in every single day and say they were in a hurry. They were never on time getting back to work. They either had more than thirty minutes, or being late was worth the discounts they received.

People will also complain when they are on a wait to be seated. "How much longer?" "Where are we on the list?" I'm sorry, I'll go ask the people eating to stop and leave so we can seat you. These guests don't understand the concept of a full restaurant. There are only so many tables. When one table leaves, you seat the next name on the list. There is no special magic that will get you seated faster. They will stand there and stare down the host like it's their fault they have to wait to eat. They finally get a table, and then sit there for forty-five minutes after they are done eating and the cycle continues. If you don't want to wait, then don't go to a restaurant when it is full.

There is also the customer who will tell their server and the manager that everything is good, and then tell the host on the way out the door that it sucked. What is the point of this? If something was really wrong, tell your server so they can fix it. I will never understand the logic in waiting until you leave to complain. It's like having surgery, and then telling the nurse as they wheel you to your car that you didn't want the surgery.

Regular customers, ones that frequently dine at the

same location, can be the biggest pain in the ass. A lot of them expect special service and free food. They think because they dine at a place five times a week that they are somehow held at a higher standard than anyone else in the restaurant. They will seat themselves, demand a certain server, call corporate on a regular basis, and complain about everything. The problem with the regular customer who likes their server is that they try to tie them up at their table like they don't have any other tables to wait on. This is a selfish behavior. Next time I'm in line at the bank, I'm going to have a ten minute conversation with the teller about my life. That will go over well.

Some regulars also expect, no matter how busy the restaurant is, that they are to never wait on anything. Their coffee better not be empty. Their food better be out in ten minutes. They better be seated at their favorite table. I had to deal with one of these fine citizens at one restaurant I worked at. This guy and his wife would come in every morning. They would send their scrambled eggs back if there was one brown spot on them. The man would tap his spoon on his coffee cup if it was empty until the server refilled it. One busy Sunday breakfast, he came up and screamed at me because his server hadn't been to the table in three minutes. Finally, the servers stopped catering to this guy, and he never returned. This might seem like a bad business decision, but to me it was a good morale decision. These employees didn't deserve to be treated like this.

I had a Canadian guest tell me once that they were going to call the President of the United States on me because my restaurant did not serve poached eggs. I could not help but laugh. That was not the proper response, as they went to my boss to complain about me. I would have rather they called the President.

My most famous customer interaction came with a gentleman who told me that I didn't know how to do my job, and he was never coming back. This guy came in every

Thursday night with a bunch of people and they were never satisfied. They tried to get free food from the server and ran them up and down until they couldn't stand. This particular night they actually had a legitimate complaint. I was in the back fixing it for them when their server told me they wanted me at the table now. After the guy said he was never coming back, I said "Fine, you don't have to eat here." He then told me to kiss his ass. When he got home, he called my boss and told him he would never return until I got fired. He was back the very next week. He did get his wish, however it was almost a year later.

The pervert regular is perhaps the most disturbing. This ladies man will sit at the bar or a counter just to hit on the waitresses or bartenders. Most of them are old and dirty. I had a colleague tell me that one of his old pervert customers offered his server $150 for a blow job. If she wouldn't do it, he would pay her $100 to find someone else to do it and pay that girl $50. Do people do this at Wal-Mart? Do they hang out and talk to the same cashier for hours every day? What is it with restaurants? Wal-Mart wouldn't put up with it. Restaurants do.

Lastly, we have our poor tippers. In some states, servers get paid only $2.13 an hour. They make their money on tips. Some people think you tip one dollar for every person at the table. This is unacceptable. I've seen two people order forty dollars worth of food and tip their server two dollars. The server should have received eight dollars at a twenty percent tip rate. I could understand if they received poor service, but these people ran the server all over the restaurant. Some people don't even tip at all. If you can't afford to tip, or refuse to tip, then don't go out to eat.

I feel really sorry for servers at 24 hour establishments. I've never seen servers treated so rudely in my life. Drunk people will come in, be loud, fight, complain, and then leave a piece of gum for a tip. I think after midnight, a 20% gratuity should automatically be added to the check. Some people think this should be the norm for any check. Of course this could confuse customers, as it did for one of "Big Guy" Shaun McKeown's tables.

"Who ordered eighteen dollars of grat-U-ity? Who ordered it," said his customer.

There are great customers that do go to restaurants. Sadly, there aren't that many. I've met great regulars. I've met super tippers. I've met people that will wait forty minutes for food and understand it's because we are busy. If all customers acted this way, you know like human beings, a restaurant might not be all that bad of a place to work.

Chapter 3
Guest Satisfaction Ratings

Have you ever received a survey while dining out? Did you have a pretty good experience and give the restaurant a four out of five? Chances are you just got your server in trouble. Many restaurants make or break their satisfaction numbers on these surveys, and a lot of them only count the survey as "good" if they receive a five out of five.

The last restaurant I worked at, we would get about fifty surveys a month. We would have around twelve thousand customers a month, so our rating would be based on roughly 0.4% of our customer base. Doesn't seem like the number would be accurate at all, yet this is one of the reasons I got fired. If you want accurate guest satisfaction ratings with this system, survey every guest, and take an average of their one through five ratings. People think four out of five is good. Restaurants don't. It's five or nothing.

Some customers will give you a bad rating just because they can never be satisfied. Some don't understand the system. I had one survey that was a three out of five, yet the comment said that "the server and food were outstanding." Even with that great comment, the survey counted as a zero against our average.

Two questions at one particular restaurant really bothered me. They were "Are you likely to return" and "Are you likely to recommend." I understand the importance of these questions, but it was the choices the customer had to choose from that were the problem. They could pick: 1. "Definitely not." 2. "Probably not." 3. "Might or might not." 4. "Probably." 5. "Definitely." Are you kidding me? How about a yes or no? These questions made up 67% of the score at this restaurant, and only choice "Definitely" counted as anything good. You are asking for a low score when 80% of the choices are bad.

When I go out to eat I either have a great experience or

a bad experience. Why not have the surveys ask that? Was your experience great? Yes or no? Was your server great? Yes or no? Food? If they put no, then you can drill down as to why they felt it was a bad experience. Not only would this give you a fairer score, it would also help guest satisfaction as a whole. I would be getting a lot of threes and fours and then forced to fix problems that weren't there because the guest didn't understand the system.

God forbid you tell them to give you fives if they are completely satisfied. That's a no-no. If the guest isn't educated on the scoring system, you will not get accurate results. If you only survey 0.4% of your guests you will not get accurate results. The system is broken in some restaurants.

Chapter 4
Servers

Servers have the toughest job in the business. They are constantly moving and their brain has to be running a mile a minute to remember everything. Servers are not treated well by management in a lot of restaurants. If a customer complains on the service, well the customer is always right. I wrote up a particular server because the customer chewed me out about his poor service. After researching, I realized the customer was a jerk and had actually received great service. What I did was not fair to the server. I rectified the situation by throwing away the write-up, but how did that server feel after my initial conversation? He probably wanted to tell me to go fuck myself.

Suggestive selling is big in restaurants, and it all lies on the shoulders of the servers. Suggestive selling is suggesting certain items that a guest might not order on their own, hoping that they will then order it. Servers are highly responsible for their drink sales, whether it be a soda, tea, or alcohol. If the customer orders water it is no profit to the company. This is the problem right here. Healthy people drink water. They come in to the restaurant already knowing they want water. You are not going to talk this person into anything else. The server can suggest the entire menu of drinks, but if they bring out four waters to the table, they then have a manager on their back. It isn't fair. I'm not saying servers shouldn't suggestive sell, because it does work. You can upgrade someone from a regular iced tea to a strawberry iced tea very easily. Managers just need to lay off the servers who do suggestive sell but bring water anyway.

Servers are constantly being watched. Whether it's by their manager, secret shoppers, excise, or corporate visits, they are the ones being nitpicked. I was taught to listen to the servers to make sure they were suggestive selling. How would you perform at your job if someone was constantly looking over your shoulder? All I was doing was making them nervous or pissed off.

In some restaurants, servers have to bus and clean their own sections. How can you yell at a server when one of their tables needs refills because they are cleaning off a table? It is very hard when you are busy to give great service and bus your own tables. I feel sorry for servers who have to do this on a regular basis. You have to spend money to make money but some corporate head honchos don't understand this. All that matters is labor dollars. If you hire a busser, you will have a cleaner restaurant, and your servers only have to worry about satisfying their customers. This will lead to higher guest satisfaction, in turn raising your sales and lowering your labor percentage even with a busser on the clock. It doesn't take a genius to figure that out. Sadly, some companies will continue to micromanage labor and not let the restaurant spend money to grow sales. Instead, they will have a sweaty nasty looking server waiting on their guests because they have been running around all day trying to keep up with the guests and cleaning the tables. A few restaurants even have the servers clean the dirty dishes. That is beyond wrong.

After a hard day's work serving your guests for eight hours, you would be ready to go home, would you not? A server has to stay and roll silverware before they go home. I know this needs to be done, but will someone invent a silverware rolling machine already? It can't be that difficult. Pop a clean fork, spoon and knife into a machine, have it wrap it in a napkin, and you're done. If I had the know-how I would invent this myself. I could retire off of that because I'm sure every restaurant would invest in those to get their servers off the clock faster.

Servers will take the brunt of the beating from the customer when something is wrong with their food. This happens a lot, and is very stressful to the server. Even with tips, I think servers are underpaid. They are the face of the restaurant, and they have to put up with every problem faced whether they caused it or not.

While I believe that the best servers make more money than the best cooks, there are days when you work and go home with hardly any money. When I was a server, I worked an 11-8 shift one day and only had four tables. After 9 hours of work I went home with $13. It's hard to depend on cash every day, and it's even harder to save it when it's in your pocket every day.

A server can make a lot of mistakes, especially the new ones. Let's go through the steps a server normally uses when waiting on a guest. First, they have to greet the table. This is where they offer their specific bar drink or upsell drink. They also are to offer an appetizer. If the customer is not ready to order, the server will go get the drinks, put in the appetizer order, and come back to the table with the drinks. As they take the order, they are to also suggestive sell anything they can think of. After sending the order to the kitchen, the server has to get salads, bread, and cold side items out to the customer while watching for their drinks to be empty. The server is supposed to remove the empty salad bowls before their entrées are served. When the food is ready, the server gathers it together and runs it out to the table, distributing each order to each guest. They check back to make sure everything is great, and bring the table anything else they need. It's at this point where most restaurants require the server to suggest a specific dessert. After the meal, the server clears all dishes and brings the dessert if ordered. This all seems easy enough, right? That's just one table. Imagine having to juggle all these steps with four or five tables at a time. Do cashiers at Wal-Mart ring out four or five customers at a time? No, because that would be absurd. It's no wonder servers make so many mistakes.

We all make mistakes every single day, but a server is supposed to be perfect. They should never mess up an order. They should never spill a drink. They should never forget an item. Managers can be pretty unforgiving when a server angers a customer. It's a poor way to treat your face of the restaurant. I am guilty of this on hundreds of occasions because shit rolls downhill. It's not right. Most restaurants would suffer immensely if their top four servers quit. Managers and customers need to be more forgiving. We all make mistakes at our job. I completely understand why some of my servers disliked me.

"Not everyone thinks about the servers and what we go through. We deal with the mean people and try to make everything absolutely perfect for them, but you don't see the people running to the back yelling at the cooks. It's all on us and the more the order is messed up, the more our tip shrinks."

- Kayla Akers, server

Chapter 5
Double-Standards

One of my fellow General Managers was fired for sleeping with a subordinate. This same subordinate was rumored to have had sex with another one of her bosses. That guy got promoted. Twice.

Double-standards like this happen all the time in the restaurant business. Whether it's at the top of the corporate ladder or in the restaurant, no one rule applies to everyone. The top employees can miss work more than an average employee. I've seen, and shamefully taken part in, a great employee with a terrible attendance record not lose their job. I've also fired untalented employees with two or three absences. That's how we were taught. Do not lose your good people. I had a server tell me, and she was half-joking, that "You'll never fire me." She was right. It didn't matter what she did, she was too valuable to me and I would never fire her. When we hold people to different standards, not only is it discrimination, but it lowers employee morale in the restaurant. The handbook at this particular restaurant was very vague on attendance termination. It was left to "the discretion of the General Manager." Let me translate that. Fire who you want and keep who you want. There should be a clear attendance policy that everyone is held accountable for.

One of the companies I worked for had a period of time where all raises were frozen. This was tough on me and I lost some good employees to other high paying jobs. The company expected our employees to perform at a high standard and not be rewarded for it just to hit a budget number. I know for a fact that a couple managers got raises during this period. If that's not a double-standard then I don't know what is.

One restaurant I was at, I was not allowed to give my managers vacations over holidays. It made sense because they are our busiest times. One year, I was told I could give a manager a vacation over Christmas because they had too many days left. My other managers were upset, and rightfully so. I had no way to justify this to them. Just a simple case of not all rules apply to everyone.

I worked with a manager who was fired for being late to open the restaurant. Another manager called off at least ten times and was never fired. Granted, two different General Managers handled each case separately, but there should be the same standards for everyone. Firing a manager who shows up to work every day but was late once, and letting one stay who calls off all the time is bullshit. In my opinion either fire both or neither. You can't treat people differently. I know it's human nature, but it's not right.

I worked for a manager once who had me make up two days I missed because I was sick. I didn't have a problem with it. I missed work, I'll make it up. However, this same manager let one of my coworkers miss four days with an illness and they didn't have to make up one of them. I didn't complain, but I was pissed. Who wouldn't be? I'm sure I've made decisions similar that have pissed people off. It gets instilled in your blood in this business. I probably have a lot of apologizing to do.

Numbers on paper are all that is important in this business. How you get there is another double-standard. I pride myself on doing things the right way. If corporate wanted it done a certain way, then that's how it was done in my restaurant. Whether my numbers were good or bad, I knew there were legit. Corporate will turn a blind eye to a restaurant with outstanding numbers who aren't getting them the right way. I've known managers to call in surveys for their restaurant. I've been told of managers who cheat when counting their inventory. There are unethical ways around labor cost. The #1 restaurant in my area had long term servers that would give away free food to regulars. Everyone knows about it, but nobody cares because their sales were high. I knew if corporate was to walk in my restaurant they would see everything (mostly) being done the way they wanted it. In the end it didn't matter, because all they cared about were numbers on a paper.

"I feel unappreciated because I do work beyond my duties and get no recognition for it. I'm only acknowledged if I make a mistake."

-   Anonymous   Current
    Manager

Chapter 6
Corporate

The corporate office normally has high expectations. For everything. Whether it's food cost, bar mix, labor cost, sales, profits, guest satisfaction, or controllable expenses, you better have them all in line.

A good corporation, no matter what industry, will focus on your successes and build off of that. In the restaurant industry, a lot of companies focus on the negative. I worked for two of those companies. You could have good food cost, good profits, but bad labor, and be on an outlier list. There were outlier lists for everything.

Working with a corporate office also means there are things out of your control. The last building I worked in had a bad A/C unit. During July and August, it would get over 100 degrees in the kitchen. I notified corporate facilities numerous times. Nothing was ever done. My cooks were so sweaty that they looked like they jumped in a pool. Can any of you imagine working on a hot grill for eight hours straight in a kitchen that hot? It was unbelievable. It is very hard to perform your job well in that environment. The heat spread to the dining room, so the customers had another thing to complain about. Servers were going to tables with wet nasty hair. It was almost 80 degrees in the dining room.

When corporate gets involved with a guest complaint, it can be very frustrating. One customer was so upset, that I took care of his entire meal and gave him $20 in vouchers for his next visit. He went home and called corporate and they sent him $25 more. I emailed the lady that sent the money and politely asked that before she sends out money to guests maybe she should research the issue with the restaurant first. With the vouchers and the cost of the bill I had already given this guy around $45. Now he has received around $70 in compensation. I was told to apologize for sending that e-mail. The $25 that the lady at corporate sent this man hit my restaurant's profit statement.

Early in my career, the restaurant I was serving at was being remodeled. The corporate office sent a trainer out to retrain us on the basics of the company and our jobs. This guy was rude and negative. We had to wait on him and he pointed out every mistake we made. This is not a way to motivate your staff for a grand reopening.

The last restaurant I worked at also had a remodeling. I went through the remodel remembering what this guy did for us at my previous job. I ran the training and teaching sessions with positivity and tried to get my staff excited for the upcoming changes. I did all this with two kidney stones. Three weeks and a surgery later, I was fired. After all the hard work I did during the remodel and reopen, corporate decided I was no longer fit to run the restaurant I had for the past four plus years.

The reason I was given was that I didn't hit my ninety day performance action plan that was laid out in November 2011. This was true, however the Wednesday before I was fired my boss told me that even though I didn't hit the plan, I was not getting fired. In fact, he was giving me a manager to train. That Sunday night he emailed saying there was a mandatory manager meeting Monday at 12:30. Monday is one of my days off. I drove my thirty-five minutes to work that day so he could fire me on my day off.

"It says a lot about a business when one will leave what is near to the top of the chain of command and literally go to being a temporary employee just to get out of that field. I would wager that in the restaurant business you will find a higher percentage of alcoholism and depression than any other career. Why? Because you are in a zero accountability environment. No customer has any sort of barrier to doing whatever they want to verbally abuse the people that serve them. The upper echelon in the food service field is NOT actually in the food service business. They tout phrases like corporate family and brand loyalty but that's only an upward trend as I have seen firsthand that no such loyalty or sense of family exists

of them towards the people actually working down in the trenches."

- John Mark Schmidt,
former Kitchen Manager

Chapter 7
Schedules

Lots of industries have tough schedules that you have to work. Restaurants are right up there with the worst of them. The busy times for restaurants are when the rest of the world is off of work. This leaves us working weekends, holidays, and nights. It's hard to have a family life when you have to work these shifts.

I cringe every time I drive by a restaurant that says it is open on Thanksgiving or Christmas. These restaurants are doing anything they can to make sales at the cost of their employees' personal lives. Those two days, nobody should be working. This goes for any industry. People need time with their families. Working on Thanksgiving or Christmas has to suck. I do appreciate that some of these restaurants have the shifts as volunteer only, but it is not the case everywhere. I worked at a restaurant where we had to sign up for Thanksgiving. We had the choice of AM or PM. Everyone had to work. I chose AM. I was scheduled PM.

The day after Thanksgiving, or Black Friday, is a busy day for restaurants. All the lucky people that don't have to work are out shopping and eating. Restaurants have to overstaff to compensate for this. Many restaurant employees, who don't make much money, miss out on good Christmas deals for their families.

I've worked with many parents who miss their kids' sports games because they have to work nights or weekends. It's very easy to have a poor quality of life when working at a restaurant. I wish there was a solution for this, but I guess when you work at a restaurant you know what you are getting yourself into.

Husbands and wives who work at the same restaurant rarely get the same schedule. It is very hard to do when you have to staff certain ways. I've had to tell some of these people that I can't schedule them together. It really sucks. With one of the couples, the wife worked day shift and the husband worked nights. They never saw each other.

Some restaurants work their managers six days a week. I did it for one month and it killed me. I couldn't imagine doing it every week. People deserve two days off a week, unless they are volunteering for extra hours. Most managers make salary and don't get extra pay for working six days.

"What most people don't realize is that managers are on salary. That means that if you work thirty hours, you get paid for fifty. Now as a matter of fact that did happen a handful of times in the years I was a manager. Aside from that I never, and I do mean never, worked a regular week where I only logged in fifty hours. So your home life is suffering no matter what. And should someone not show up for work? Well that means that the other manager stays over because there is no one else. Or say someone is sick? Looks like that manager pulls a six day week. Someone on vacation? Fifteen to twenty day stretches are not outside the norm for a manager. Your schedule is really just a matter of theory rather than fact.

As a kitchen manager I regularly pulled twenty hour shifts to finish up work that needed to be done that I wasn't able to get to in the course of the rest of the week. That means yes, I went in at 7:00 AM and did not leave until 3:00 AM the next day. Because the expectation of the corporate management was that these things could be done throughout the shift. Though you could never allot manpower to do it as there was always some unreasonable benchmark to be made. Less manpower and higher sales. A spotless dining room with no cleaning crew other than servers who are making $2.13 an hour and still have to take care of customers as well as prepare things in the back of the house for business trends throughout the day. See where this is going?

And people still seem to be surprised at the level of stress and failed marriages/relationships and instances of alcoholism that crops up in the food service management pool. When you are working as a restaurant manager, your life really revolves around being available and on call no matter what. Your home life takes a second seat because there is no 'off' time on your schedule. You are never unavailable, it's just a matter of when someone is going to call you in."

- John Mark Schmidt,
  former Kitchen Manager

Chapter 8
Bad Hires

I made some terrible hires. I'm sure all managers have. You have a great interview with someone, you hire them, and then the person who shows up to work has a completely different personality then the one you hired.

Keeping turnover down is a big responsibility of a General Manager. In fact, at one point it affected 10% of my bonus. So what do you do with a bad hire? You try to make them into a good employee. Nine times out of ten it doesn't work. They will either ruin a guest's experience or drag down morale.

I hired a server based on a recommendation from someone I already had on staff. The interview went well. Two weeks later, I realized he was a psycho. He was always screaming at his coworkers. Finally, after he went off on an Assistant Manager, I had to fire him. He proceeded to tell me that I was "a little bitch" and if he ever saw me in the street he would "kick my fuckin' ass." Luckily, I never saw him in the street. I did, however, call the police.

Some bad hires never leave. You're not supposed to fire someone "just because", but there are those that can walk the fine line where they don't lose their job. Ten years later, you're wondering why this person still works here. These "lifers" will kill your staff morale. They usually are below average performers and bitch about everything. The kicker is the regulars usually love this person.

Hire the wrong person as a bartender and you might as well stop selling alcohol. We've all seen the over pour. Add those up over a week. Over a month. A year. You get the point. These people cost restaurants thousands of dollars in alcohol waste. Then when a good bartender comes in and makes the drink correctly, the customer gets pissed off because they didn't get as much alcohol as they did from the other person.

Manager's fall into the "desperate hire" trap. In a flash, your restaurant can become understaffed. Instead of hiring talent, you hire anybody that walks in the door to fill your staff. These people don't work out, they quit, and the cycle continues. This is hell for your core staff, because they are the ones dealing with the revolving door and working six days a week because you are don't have enough people. Once you get in this cycle, it's a hard one to get out of. I've been through many of these turnover cycles, and it's one reason I wanted to get out of the restaurant business. Being short staffed easily contributed to my receding hairline.

"Turnover is always high in the restaurant business. People hate coming to work to cover other people's job, so they quit because the job sucks. The job sucks so bad because the turnover is always so high. It's a vicious cycle."

- Andrew   Wiseman,
  former grill cook

Chapter 9
Never Again

I spent too many years of my life busting my butt for restaurants that didn't really care about me. Perhaps my firing was a blessing. Without it, I may have been stuck in the industry for many years to come. I have taken a vow to never work in a restaurant again.

Some of you may think I'm a bitter idiot who deserved to be fired. That's fine. I have a middle finger with your name on it. Seriously, though, if you enjoy working in restaurants then continue to do it. There are good restaurant companies out there. With that said I do believe that the customers and their behaviors will never change. The way things are done to satisfy these customers will not change. Stress levels will not be lowered. If you are immune to all of this, then I envy you.

This was my avenue to speak my mind now that I finally can. I worked with a lot of great people in this industry. For the most part, the people working in restaurants are not the problem. I feel sorry for people that put up with the things I covered day in and day out. I feel sorry that I contributed to stress levels at times. I miss all the good people I worked with. I even miss a lot of the customers.

I gave my all to a certain restaurant company and was forced out by a boss with a chip on his shoulder. I am angry that he lied to me about being fired. I am angry how he treated me on my "firing day." I can't believe that corporate backs him and ignores all the facts I presented to them. I had postponed surgery for kidney stones that were too big to piss out and were shutting down my kidneys. I put off that surgery for the company, and now I regret the decision. I was very good at my job. Now, it's time to find something else I'm good at, because working in a restaurant sucks.

www.ingramcontent.com/pod-product-compliance
Lightning Source LLC
Chambersburg PA
CBHW060607030426
42337CB00019B/3646